A. Meiappane
V. Premanand

CAPTCHA as Graphical Passwords - A New Security Primitive

A. Meiappane
V. Premanand

CAPTCHA as Graphical Passwords - A New Security Primitive

Based on Hard AI Problems

Scholar's Press

Impressum / Imprint
Bibliografische Information der Deutschen Nationalbibliothek: Die Deutsche Nationalbibliothek verzeichnet diese Publikation in der Deutschen Nationalbibliografie; detaillierte bibliografische Daten sind im Internet über http://dnb.d-nb.de abrufbar.
Alle in diesem Buch genannten Marken und Produktnamen unterliegen warenzeichen-, marken- oder patentrechtlichem Schutz bzw. sind Warenzeichen oder eingetragene Warenzeichen der jeweiligen Inhaber. Die Wiedergabe von Marken, Produktnamen, Gebrauchsnamen, Handelsnamen, Warenbezeichnungen u.s.w. in diesem Werk berechtigt auch ohne besondere Kennzeichnung nicht zu der Annahme, dass solche Namen im Sinne der Warenzeichen- und Markenschutzgesetzgebung als frei zu betrachten wären und daher von jedermann benutzt werden dürften.

Bibliographic information published by the Deutsche Nationalbibliothek: The Deutsche Nationalbibliothek lists this publication in the Deutsche Nationalbibliografie; detailed bibliographic data are available in the Internet at http://dnb.d-nb.de.
Any brand names and product names mentioned in this book are subject to trademark, brand or patent protection and are trademarks or registered trademarks of their respective holders. The use of brand names, product names, common names, trade names, product descriptions etc. even without a particular marking in this work is in no way to be construed to mean that such names may be regarded as unrestricted in respect of trademark and brand protection legislation and could thus be used by anyone.

Coverbild / Cover image: www.ingimage.com

Verlag / Publisher:
Scholar's Press
ist ein Imprint der / is a trademark of
OmniScriptum GmbH & Co. KG
Heinrich-Böcking-Str. 6-8, 66121 Saarbrücken, Deutschland / Germany
Email: info@scholars-press.com

Herstellung: siehe letzte Seite /
Printed at: see last page
ISBN: 978-3-639-76923-4

Copyright © 2015 OmniScriptum GmbH & Co. KG
Alle Rechte vorbehalten. / All rights reserved. Saarbrücken 2015

ACKNOWLEDGEMENT

I express my sincere thanks to our Chairman and Managing Director **Shri. M. DHANASEKARAN** for all his encouragement and moral support. I thank our Vice Chairman **Shri. V. SUGUMARAN** and Secretary **Dr. K. NARAYANASAMY** for his support and encouragement.

It gives me great ecstasy of pleasure to convey my deep and sincere thanks to our Principal **Dr. S. MALARKKAN**, for giving constant motivation in succeeding my goal. With profoundness I would like to express my sincere thanks to **Dr. K.B. JAYARRAMAN**, Head of the Department, Computer Science Engineering, for his kindness in extending the infrastructural facilities to carry out my project work successfully.

I extend my sincere and heartfelt thanks to my guide **Dr. A. MEIAPPANE**, Associate Professor, Department of Information technology, for providing the right ambience for carrying out this work and his valuable guidance and suggestions for my project work. I thank him for the continuous encouragement and the interest shown on me to bring out my project work at this stage and also for providing the freedom that I needed and wanted.

I would like to express my gratitude to all teaching and non-teaching staff members of our Department. And above all, the blessings of the **Almighty** has kept up my spirit and enabled me to complete my study successfully.

ABSTRACT

Many security primitives are based on hard mathematical problems. Using hard AI problems for security is emerging as an exciting new paradigm, but has been underexplored. In this project, we present a new security primitive based on hard AI problems, namely, a novel family of graphical password systems built on top of Captcha technology, which we call Captcha as graphical passwords (CaRP). CaRP is both a Captcha and a graphical password scheme.

CaRP addresses a number of security problems altogether, such as online guessing attacks, relay attacks, and, if combined with dual-view technologies, shoulder-surfing attacks. Notably, a CaRP password can be found only probabilistically by automatic online guessing attacks even if the password is in the search set. CaRP also offers a novel approach to address the well-known image hotspot problem in popular graphical password systems, such as PassPoints that often leads to weak password choices. CaRP is not a panacea, but it offers reasonable security and usability and appears to fit well with some practical applications for improving online security.

ii

TABLE OF CONTENTS

v

LIST OF FIGURES

LIST OF FLOW CHARTS

LIST OF ABBREVATIONS

CAPTCHA	Completely Automated Public Turing test to tell Computers and Humans Apart
CaRP	Captcha as gRaphical Password
AI	Artificial Intelligence
CPA	Choosen Pixel Attack
PDA	Personal Digital Assistant

CHAPTER-1

INTRODUCTION

A fundamental task in security is to create cryptographic primitives based on hard mathematical problems that are computationally intractable. For example, the problem of integer factorization is fundamental to the RSA public-key cryptosystem and the Rabin encryption. The discrete logarithm problem is fundamental to the ElGamal encryption, the Diffie- Hellman key exchange, the Digital Signature Algorithm, the elliptic curve cryptography and so on. Using hard AI (Artificial Intelligence) problems for security, initially proposed in, is an exciting new paradigm. Under this paradigm, the most notable primitive invented is Captcha, which distinguishes human users from computers by presenting a challenge, i.e., a puzzle, beyond the capability of computers but easy for humans. Captcha is now a standard Internet security technique to protect online email and other services from being abused by bots.

However, this new paradigm has achieved just a limited success as compared with the cryptographic primitives based on hard math problems and their wide applications. Is it possible to create any new security primitive based on hard AI problems? This is a challenging and interesting open problem. In this paper, we introduce a new security primitive based on hard AI problems, namely, a novel family of graphical password systems integrating Captcha technology, which we call *CaRP (Captcha as gRaphical Passwords)*. CaRP is click-based graphical passwords, where a sequence of clicks on an image is used to derive a password. Unlike other click-based graphical passwords, images used in CaRP are Captcha challenges, and a new CaRP image is generated for every login attempt. The notion of CaRP is simple but generic. CaRP can have multiple instantiations. In theory, any Captcha scheme relying on multiple-object classification can be converted to a CaRP scheme. We present exemplary CaRPs built on both text Captcha and image-recognition Captcha. One of them is a text CaRP wherein a password is a sequence of characters like a text password, but entered by clicking the right character sequence on CaRP images.

1.1 COMMON DEFINITIONS OF CAPTCHA

An effective CAPTCHA should differentiate the humans from bots and even an effective program can't break these tests, so the common definitions are:

1. Easily tackled by people

2. Easily created and asserted, but

3. The computer programs can't solve easily.

For the past 14 years many techniques over CAPTCHA have been proposed, where the security have been emerged day by day. An effective CAPTCHA must be a basic thing for the user to solve with involving a basic knowledge of the user so that most of the users passes these tests and the user's time is not wasted in solving these CAPTCHA. Since a user can pass through these CAPTCHA easily but it is intractable for the computer programs because the basic knowledge is been used and it is very costly to design the systems to break these CAPTCHA than using human resources.

The commonly used CAPTCHA are Visual CAPTCHA where the text (or) image is been muddled by changing the visual by the addition of some irregular fluctuations and distortion. Thus the challenge here is to design the muddling of visuals which is also easy for the users and they are not discouraged from attempting a CAPTCHA, yet making it too hard for the computer's vision algorithm to pass through. The major types of captcha are

    I.   Visual based CAPTCHA

    II.   Non-Visual based CAPTCHA

    III.   Feature based CAPTCHA

    IV.   Riddle based CAPTCHA

1.2 VISUAL BASED CAPTCHA

The commonly used CAPTCHA are Visual CAPTCHA where the text (or) image is been muddled by changing the visual by the addition of some irregular fluctuations and distortion. Thus the challenge here is to design the muddling of visuals which is also easy for the users and they are not discouraged from attempting a CAPTCHA, yet making it too hard for the computer's vision algorithm to pass through.

1.1.1 Text based CAPTCHA

A text based CAPTCHA is an interesting form of user interface where the point of recognition comes under reading based technique composed of English characters and Arabic numerals which are generated randomly in a distorted manner which is entered by the user in a text – box or rotating the

2

texts in a random manner in a form of equation or a text with symbols and noise in small variations in fonts.

Figure 1: A typical text based CAPTCHA

Thus we make the text based CAPTCHA is easy to solve by humans but difficult for the computer programs because of the distortion, noise, color aspects of the visuals (Ahn,L. von et al, 2003, Mukta Rao et al, 2012). The distortion is been done vertically and horizontally thus the letter is been appeared twisted out of shape (Xiao Ling-ZI et al, 2012) which becomes more difficult for the computer programs to identify.

Figure 2: Handwritten CAPTCHA   Figure 3: reCAPTCHA

1.1.2 Image based CAPTCHA

Graphical CAPTCHA are the test challenges where the user must identify some images which have some similarity. They are given in the form of visual puzzles so that the user must identify the

3

image and type the text below (or) identify the text and click the image below. Other approach is that the user must find a common feature among some set of images.

(i) Naming the images

The images which have similarities will be given in a grid so that the user must identify the set of images and type the common word from the images (figure 4). In this figure 4 the common term is astronaut. But here the user may confuse with the images and the guessing may be of a similar synonym which may go wrong. So the CAPTCHA must be provided by hints to the user which makes the system a bit complicated.

Figure 4: Naming the Images

(ii) Distinguishing the images

This type presents two sets of images to the user, each set contains three images describes same subject or different ones. The user must determine whether the images having same subject or not. For example three different images of table and other three images of a cat, but polysemy may be a problem here.

4

(iii)Identifying the oddity

Here a grid containing images of same subject, but only one image will be given different (odd image). The user must identify the odd image to pass the test (Figure 5). Here misspelling of words is not a problem, because the user is just going to click on the odd image. Polysemy may be a problem for here too , example a rat and a pointing device of a computer gives a same word 'mouse' which occurs in rare cases.

Figure 5: Identifying the oddity

(iv)Identify the image

In this type a grid containing set of images, and name of a particular image is given above, the user have to identify the image name and should click on the identified image. The user should just click on the particular image given on top of the grid so it is simpler than other image CAPTCHA technique. But the coexistence of numerous conceivable implications for a word may be a problem because two images of denoting a same word may confuse the user which occurs in rare case.

Figure 6: Identify the image

5

1.3 NON –VISUAL BASED CAPTCHA

The audio CAPTCHA is an example for a non-visual based CAPTCHA which is based on sound systems which is been designed for the users who are unable to see (Physically challenged). In this type the CAPTCHA comes with an audio - clip consisting of a spoken word of a human which is a downloadable content. The user should play the audio content and type in the given text – box.

The audio - CAPTCHA differentiates the computer bots and humans by recognizing the spoken language. The CAPTCHA consists of chosen sequence of letters and digits which is randomly spelled by a sound clip. Then the sound clip is been provided by a distortion and then presented to the user to identify and enter the right number or word.

Figure 7: Audio Captcha

1.4 FEATURE BASED CAPTCHA

A video CAPTCHA is referred as feature based CAPTCHA, which is a newer technique but very rarely seen in internet In this system 3 specific words are given in a running video format having common property with other words (say red colored words) so the user should identify the specified words from the moving words and type in given text box

6

Figure 8: Video based CAPTCHA

For a user to pass the CAPTCHA challenge, they must view a short video and enter the described tags for it. More than 60% of users say that a video CAPTCHA is "More Enjoyable" than other CAPTCHA methods because it is comfortable on human's eyes and more secure for bots.

Figure 9: A simple nuCAPTCHA

Figure 10: NuCAPTCHA Moving letters

1.5 RIDDLE BASED CAPTCHA

In a riddle based CAPTCHA an image is divided into lumps so that the user should be able to combine these lumps by drag and drop format and replicate the original image to pass the CAPTCHA test. Generally the humans can perform this task well but the bots can't resulting in highly secured system. The main advantage is this system is a language independent so that any user can pass the test.

Figure 11: Riddle based CAPTCHA

8

CHAPTER-2

LITERATURE SURVEY

2.1 INTRODUCTION

A literature review is an objective, critical summary of published research literature relevant to a topic under consideration for research. Its purpose is to create familiarity with current thinking and research on a particular topic, and may justify future research into a previously overlooked or understudied area.

2.2 Graphical Passwords: Learning from the First Twelve Years (R. Biddle et al, 2012)

Starting around 1999, a great many graphical password schemes have been proposed as alternatives to text-based password authentication. (R. Biddle et al, 2012) provide a comprehensive overview of published research in the area, covering both usability and security aspects, as well as system evaluation. The paper first catalogues existing approaches, highlighting novel features of selected schemes and identifying key usability or security advantages. Then review usability requirements for knowledge-based authentication as they apply to graphical passwords, identify security threats that such systems must address and review known attacks, discuss methodological issues related to empirical evaluation, and identify areas for further research and improved methodology.

2.3 The Design And Analysis Of Graphical Passwords (Jermyn A. Mayer et al, 1999)

In this paper (Jermyn A. Mayer et al, 1999) propose and evaluate new graphical password schemes that exploit features of graphical input displays to achieve better security than text based passwords. Graphical input devices enable the user to decouple the position of inputs from the temporal order in which those inputs occur, and show that this decoupling can be used to generate password schemes with substantially larger (memorable) password spaces. In order to evaluate the security of one of our schemes, devise a novel way to capture a subset of the memorable" passwords that believe, is itself a contribution.

2.4 A new graphical password scheme against spyware by using CAPTCHA (L Wang et al, 2013)

CAPTCHA is used in a graphical password scheme to resist spyware. A CAPTCHA (Completely Automated Public Turing tests to tell Computers and Humans Apart) is a program that generates and grades tests that are human solvable, but are beyond the capabilities of current computer programs. CAPTCHA uses open algorithms based on hard AI problems, and has been discussed in text-based password schemes to resist dictionary attack. Innovatively, (L Wang et al, 2013) explore CAPTCHA in the context of graphical passwords to provide better protection against spyware. As long as the underlying open AI problems are not solved, CAPTCHA is a promising way to resist spyware attack in graphical password schemes. Based on this key idea, they have proposed a new graphical password scheme using CAPTCHA, designed to be strongly resistant to spyware attack, either by purely automated software or via human participation. A preliminary user study indicates that our scheme needs to improve in terms of login time and memorability.

Drawbacks: The results of experiments show that the login time and memorability is not ideal, which indicates an area for further research. Additional narrowing the time gap in the entering process and reduction of the impact of user's choice trend on security.

2.5 Pass-Go: A Proposal to Improve the Usability of Graphical Passwords (H.Tao et al, 2008)

Inspired by an old Chinese game, Go, (H.Tao et al, 2008) have designed a new graphical password scheme, Pass-Go, in which a user selects intersections on a grid as a way to input a password. While offering an extremely large full password space our scheme provides acceptable usability, as empirically demonstrated by, to the best of our knowledge, the largest user study on graphical passwords, conducted in the fall semester of 2005 in two university classes. This scheme supports most application environments and input devices, rather than being limited to small mobile devices (PDAs), and can be used to derive cryptographic keys.

Drawbacks: The Pass-Go scheme must be optimized for size and space, setting up better color combination strategies, looking for better solutions for the shoulder surfing problem etc.

2.6 PassPoints: Design and longitudinal evaluation of a graphical password system (S. Wiedenbeck et al, 2005)

Computer security depends largely on passwords to authenticate human users. However, users have difficulty remembering passwords over time if they choose a secure password, i.e. a password that is long and random. Therefore, they tend to choose short and insecure passwords. Graphical passwords, which consist of clicking on images rather than typing alphanumeric strings, may help to overcome the problem of creating secure and memorable passwords. In this paper (S. Wiedenbeck et al, 2005) describe PassPoints, a new and more secure graphical password system. Participants created and practiced either an alphanumeric or graphical password. The participants subsequently carried out three longitudinal trials to input their password over the course of 6 weeks. The results show that the graphical password users created a valid password with fewer difficulties than the alphanumeric users. However, the graphical users took longer and made more invalid password inputs than the alphanumeric users while practicing their passwords. In the longitudinal trials the two groups performed similarly on memory of their password, but the graphical group took more time to input a password.

2.7 Exploiting Predictability in Click-based Graphical Passwords (P. C. van Oorschot et al, 2011)

It provides an in-depth study of the security of click-based graphical password schemes like PassPoints (P. C. van Oorschot et al, 2011), by exploring popular points (hot-spots), and examining strategies to predict and exploit them in guessing attacks. They report on both short- and long-term user studies: one lab controlled, involving 43 users and 17 diverse images, the other a field test of 223 user accounts. It provides empirical evidence that hot-spots do exist for many images, some more so than others. It explores the use of "human-computation" (in this context, harvesting click-points from a small set of users) to predict these hot-spots. It generates two "human-seeded" attacks based on this method: one based on a first-order Markov model, another based on an independent probability model. Within 100 guesses, the first-order Markov model-based attack finds 4% of passwords in one image's data set, and 10% of passwords in a second image's data set. Our independent model-based attack finds 20% within 233 guesses in one image's data set and 36% within 231 guesses in a second image's data set. These are all for a system whose full password space has cardinality 243. They also evaluate our first-order Markov model-based attack with cross-validation of the field study data, which finds an average of 7-10% of user passwords within 3 guesses. (P. C. van Oorschot et al, 2011) also begin to

11

explore some click-order pattern attacks, which found improve on our independent model-based attacks. Our results suggest that these graphical password schemes (with parameters as originally proposed) are vulnerable to offline and online attacks, even on systems that implement conservative lock-out policies.

2.8 Click passwords under investigation (K.Golofit, 2007)

The paper explores one of the graphical authentication techniques as the possible solution to the most important problems of traditional passwords. The aim of this work is to bring together the technical (cryptological) and non-technical (psychological) awareness into the research on passwords (click passwords in this case). Security issues of any authentication mechanism (relying on knowledge) should not be considered without analysis of the human factor – since the users' human nature was identified as a source of major weaknesses of conventional authentication. (K.Golofit, 2007) deals with techniques which reduce password space and make passwords guesses feasible. Four types of pictures areas (of graphical interfaces) were investigated in order to bring to light common vulnerabilities – three of them were identified as types, which the graphical keypads should avoid. Statistics exposing strong tendentiousness in click passwords selection were presented as well. Furthermore, the paper presents a discussion on several issues of title authentication with regard to traditional passwords and other graphical techniques.

2.9 Do Background Images Improve "Draw a Secret" Graphical Passwords? (P Dunphy et al , 2007)

Draw a secret (DAS) is a representative graphical password scheme. Rigorous theoretical analysis suggests that DAS supports an overall password space larger than that of the ubiquitous textual password scheme. However, recent research suggests that DAS users tend to choose weak passwords, and their choices would render this theoretically sound scheme less secure in real life. In this paper (P Dunphy et al, 2007) investigate the novel idea of introducing background images to the DAS scheme, where users were initially supposed to draw passwords on a blank canvas overlaid with a grid. Encouraging results from our two user studies have shown that people aided with background images tended to set significantly more complicated passwords than their counterparts using the original scheme. The background images also reduced other predictable characteristics in DAS passwords such as symmetry and centering within the drawing grid, further improving the strength of the passwords. They estimate that the average strength of successfully recalled passwords in the enhanced scheme was increased over those created using the original scheme by more than 10 bits. Moreover, a positive effect was observed with respect to the memorability of the more complex passwords encouraged by the background images.

2.10 CAPTCHA: Using Hard AI Problems for Security (L von Ahn et al, 2003)

(L von Ahn et al, 2003) introduces captcha, an automated test that humans can pass, but current computer programs can't pass: any program that has high success over a captcha can be used to solve an unsolved Artificial Intelligence (AI) problem. Much like research in cryptography has had a positive impact on algorithms for factoring and discrete log, and hope that the use of hard AI problems for security purposes allows us to advance the field of Artificial Intelligence. They introduce two families of AI problems that can be used to construct captchas and we show that solutions to such problems can be used for steganography communication. Captchas based on these AI problem families, then, imply a win-win situation: either the problems remain unsolved and there is a way to differentiate humans from computers, or the problems are solved and there is a way to communicate covertly on some channels

2.11 Graphical Password Authentication Using Cued Click Points (S. Chiasson et al, 2007)

(S. Chiasson et al, 2007) propose and examine the usability and security of Cued Click Points (CCP), a cued-recall graphical password technique. Users click on one point per image for a sequence of images. The next image is based on the previous click-point. We present the results of an initial user study which revealed positive results. Performance was very good in terms of speed, accuracy, and number of errors. Users preferred CCP to PassPoints saying they thought that selecting and remembering only one point per image was easier, and that seeing each image triggered their memory of where the corresponding point was located. We also suggest that CCP provides greater security than PassPoints because the number of images increases the workload for attackers.

CHAPTER-3

SYSTEM ANALYSIS

3.1 EXISTING SYSTEM

Security primitives are based on hard mathematical problems. Using hard AI problems for security is emerging as an exciting new paradigm, but has been underexplored. A Fundamental task in security is to create cryptographic primitives based on hard mathematical problems that are computationally intractable. Using hard AI (Artificial Intelligence) problems for security, initially proposed is an exciting new paradigm. Under this paradigm, the most notable primitive invented is Captcha, which distinguishes human users from computers by presenting a challenge, i.e., a puzzle, beyond the capability of computers but easy for humans. Captcha is now a standard Internet security technique to protect online email and other services from being abused by bots. This new paradigm has achieved just a limited success as compared with the cryptographic primitives based on hard math problems and their wide applications. So the problem of making those Captcha into a security primitive is a challenge to make them non- vulnerable.

3.1.1 PASSWORD RECOGNITION SCHEMES:

In order to improve the password authentication scheme, there are many alternatives which have been proposed, e.g. Biometrics, Token based authentication, Graphical Passwords, Multiple factors scheme which uses two or more authentication schemes. Here we are going to focus on single factor scheme. There are numerous graphical password related schemes which are surveyed among which some common password systems are,

1. Recognition based systems.

2. Pure recall based systems.

3. Cued recall based systems.

In *Recognition based systems* the user can choose an image icon or a symbol from a large collection which is used for authentication. The Recognition based schemes are easy to remember but it takes a large space for storing the passwords and also requires many rounds for image recognition which makes the system tedious.

14

In *Pure recall based systems* the user needs to reproduce the passwords without any clues or hints. The best example for this scheme is Draw a Secret (DAS), where a peculiar shape is drawn in a grid. The user should reproduce the same shape to authenticate them. The main advantage is, it is simple and quick to use but it has lot of shoulder surfing problems.

In *Cued recall based systems*, the image is shown on a screen and the user should click on a few points which are pre-defined by them during registration. So the user should click on the correct regions to log in thus it is more secure and solves shoulder surfing problems.

Thus, after the usage of CAPTCHA, which is the mechanism used for BOT protection the graphical passwords came into existence to eradicate the difficulties in traditional password system. The graphical passwords are more attractive and new to the user, many systems using graphical passwords came into existence which overcomes the alphanumeric password systems. As already mentioned humans have tendency to choose weak passwords and similarly for DAS systems it is proved that humans choose mostly predictable patterns. In this thesis, we focus on the passpoint systems, usage of some similar natural images with the click based Blonder graphical system and also develop a system called Passpoints for Random Similar Images (PRSIm), where similar images are generated for each login which has exactly same passpoints where the images are partitioned as regions. Similarly, several images are generated which have same properties and the discretization grids for the system recognizes the password.

3.2 ALGORITHMS FOR VARIOUS GRAPHICAL PASSWORDS

3.2.1 TRIANGLE ALGORITHM

Triangle algorithm was developed in 2002 by Sobrado and Birget, which is mainly related with shoulder surfing problem,In this algorithm, the user is asked to select a certain number of objects from N number of proposed objects (may be a few hundred or few thousand). To authenticate, the user has to select the previously selected objects from the proposed images. But the objects are shuffled and located in different locations. The main disadvantage of this algorithm is theat the system is crowded and it is very difficult for the user to distinguish the images.

15

Figure 12. Authentication in Triangle Algorithm

3.2.2 PASSFACE ALGORITHM

Passface algorithm was developed by Brostoff and Sasse in 2000 who proposed a new graphical scheme. The user is asked to select a certain number of images of human faces from a database of images containing different human faces. During authentication the user must recognize the previously selected images from a grid where the images are shuffled. The people can select the images based on some obvious behavioral pattern so that it is easy to predict the images the system is more vulnerable on various attacks.

Figure 13. Authentication using Passface Algorithm

3.2.3 DRAW A SECRET ALGORITHM

The DAS Algorithm was proposed by Jermyn, Mayer, Monrose, Reiter, and Rubin in 1999, in which the user is allowed to draw a unique pattern password in a 2D grid during registration and stored in order of the pattern. During authentication the user redraws the pattern by touching the same points in the grid in same sequence. The main disadvantage is that the user selects weak graphical passwords which make the authentication mostly predictable and the system is vulnerable on various attacks.

16

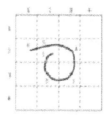

Figure 14. Authentication in Draw a secret Algorithm

3.2.4 SYUKRI ET AL ALGORITHM

The syukri et al algorithm was proposed by Syukri, Okamoto, and Mambo in 2005 which is a new graphical authentication where the user is asked to draw a signature with help of an input device and during authentication the system identifies the signature by extracting the parameters of the user's signature. The biggest advantage is that the signature is hard to reproduce and there is no memorizing of the password but the main drawback is that we cannot use a mouse to put a signature, a pen like input device is required which requires an additional hardware.

Figure 15. Authentication in Syukri et al algorithm

3.2.5 BLONDER ALGORITHM

Blonder proposed a new algorithm for graphical authentication in 1996, where an image is used and the user must click on several locations on that particular image during registration and must reselect the same locations in similar order for authentication. The image acts as a hint for the user to reproduce the password thus this system is the most convenient of the other pure recall-based schemes. The major disadvantage is the defined click areas are very small and not so accurate and it uses only simple images which are sketched and we can't use the real world images.

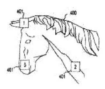

Figure 16. Authentication using Blonder Algorithm

3.3 DISADVANTAGES

1. This paradigm has achieved just a limited success as compared with the cryptographic primitives based on hard math problems and their wide applications.

2. Using hard AI (Artificial Intelligence) problems for security, initially proposed in, is an exciting new paradigm. Under this paradigm, the most notable primitive invented is Captcha, which distinguishes human users from computers by presenting a challenge.

CHAPTER-4

PROPOSED SYSTEM

We present a new security primitive based on hard AI problems, namely, a novel family of graphical password systems built on top of Captcha technology, which we call Captcha as graphical passwords (CaRP). CaRP is both a Captcha and a graphical password scheme. CaRP addresses a number of security problems altogether, such as online guessing attacks, relay attacks, and, if combined with dual-view technologies, shoulder-surfing attacks. Notably, a CaRP password can be found only probabilistically by automatic online guessing attacks even if the password is in the search set. CaRP also offers a novel approach to address the well-known image hotspot problem in popular graphical password systems, such as PassPoints that often leads to weak password choices. CaRP is not a panacea, but it offers reasonable security and usability and appears to fit well with some practical applications for improving online security. We present exemplary CaRPs built on both text Captcha and image-recognition Captcha. One of them is a text CaRP wherein a password is a sequence of characters like a text password, but entered by clicking the right character sequence on CaRP images. CaRP offers protection against online dictionary attacks on passwords, which have been for long time a major security threat for various online services. This threat is widespread and considered as a top cyber security risk. Defense against online dictionary attacks is a more subtle problem than it might appear.

4.1 PASSPOINT SYSTEM FOR CLICK BASED PASSWORDS

The Passpoints are designed to cover the limitations of the blonder algorithm consists of a high quality pictures which is rich enough to have many possible clicks.Complex images may have hundreds of memorable click points, for example 5-6 click points will make comparatively stronger passwords than alphanumeric passwords. In order to login the user has to click on the already registered click points within some tolerance points say around .25 cm in the click points. The tolerance point is needed because the user has to click the password within a certain pixel and the user cannot click accurate pixel all the time for successful login. The tolerance point is adjustable to the system and margin of error is been used for a correct recognition of the user. The passpoints are more secure than alphanumeric passwords by comparing alphanumeric passwords of length 8 over 64-bit character the number of possible passwords is $64^8 = 2.8 \times 10^{14}$ and in passpoints the maximum image size is 1024 x

752 (full screen) with a tolerance of around 20 x 20 pixels for passwords consisting of 5 clicks the password space will have a size of 2.6×10^{16}.

The Passpoints and alphanumeric passwords were compared and studied in a laboratory, to learn about the memorability of graphical passwords. The results showed that the participants from the graphical password group created valid passwords without any difficulties than the participants of alphanumeric group. But the graphical group made more errors and took more attempts in carrying out the practice as this type of password was entirely new to them. Also all the graphical password users were able to reach the learning criteria within some minutes.

4.2 STUDY OF IMAGE CHOICE

To study about the graphical use of the passwords and how it succeeds, the psychologists have studied that the images are having more focused memory than the words and sentences which was called as 'picture superiority effect'. Thus everyday images are chosen and they are made as passwords which gives a clear knowledge about learnability and memorability while using different images. The higher number of accurate passpoints is found when a constant tolerance value is given to the system and thus it gives an increased performance. Thus, it concludes that a limited knowledge is required for the use of graphical password and the average user can use this authentication system easily. In some rare cases the images with poor memorable character can also be accepted and some practice is needed because there is a chance for forgetting password because of infrequent use. As we see in using the graphical passwords we have the better results of high performance, quick learning and accuracy for people who are having poor memorability who can work easily with some practice.

4.3 PREDICTION IN GRAPHICAL PASSWORDS

There are several studies based on the prediction of the passpoints and the portions that a human focus in common. The human nature is that when asked to click any particular pixels the people will focus on a particular points of same frequency which is illustrated in figure 1 which are the click points actually clicked by the users. We can see that there are click locations which are most likely given as passwords, but the users click points reduces the entropy of the click locations. Thus the user's entropy password clicks are observed and predicted. By using Mean-shift segmentation algorithm it predicts the most likely click location with their probability values, thus the users must select the images with higher entropy of their click points.

4.4 PREDICTED VS ACTUAL CLICK LOCATIONS

Figure 17(a) Predicted Click Locations

Figure 17(b) Actual Click Locations

In the above image the users were given the images and they were made to choose their own passpoints consisting of 5 click points and were asked to re-enter, the passpoints which has been re-entered is been taken into account. The same image is been predicted by using mean-shift segmentation algorithm with having 10 pixels of tolerance for both cases of 400 x 600 pixels image. The system predicted the points with 80% accuracy for a normal image having high entropy value. The entropy value of the image, the accuracy percentage, and increased number of click points decides the strength of the password. Thus only after 31^5 ($\approx 2.8 \cdot 10^6$) iterations we can crack a user's image password. From here we can define that an image which has more number of clicks and less entropy value is more secure. By using many advanced algorithms the passpoints are ben predicted

4.5 ADVANTAGES:

1.   It offers reasonable security and usability and appears to fit well with some practical applications for improving online security.

2.   This threat is widespread and considered as a top cyber security risk. Defense against online dictionary attacks is a more subtle problem than it might appear.

CHAPTER-5

HARDWARE & SOFTWARE REQUIREMENTS

5.1 HARDWARE REQUIREMENTS:

System   :   Pentium IV 2.4 GHz.

Hard Disk   :   250 GB.

Monitor   :   15 VGA Color.

RAM   :   1 GB.

5.2 SOFTWARE REQUIREMENTS:

Operating system   :   Windows XP Professional.

Coding Language   :   Java (Jdk 1.6) with Servlet and JSP.

Database   :   My-SQL 5.0.

Server   :   Tomcat 7.0.

IDE   :   Eclipse 3.6.

CHAPTER-6

PROJECT DESCRIPTION

CaRP offers protection against online dictionary attacks on passwords, which have been for long time a major security threat for various online services. This threat is widespread and considered as a top cyber security risk. Defense against online dictionary attacks is a more subtle problem than it might appear. Intuitive countermeasures such as throttling logon attempts do not work well for two reasons:

1) It causes denial-of-service attacks (which were exploited to lock highest bidders out in final minutes of eBay auctions) and incurs expensive helpdesk costs for account reactivation.

2) It is vulnerable to global password attacks whereby adversaries intend to break into any account rather than a specific one, and thus try each password candidate on multiple accounts and ensure that the number of trials on each account is below the threshold to avoid triggering account lockout.

CaRP also offers protection against relay attacks, an increasing threat to bypass Captchas protection, wherein Captcha challenges are relayed to humans to solve. Koobface was a relay attack to bypass Facebook's Captcha in creating new accounts. CaRP is robust to shoulder-surfing attacks if combined with dual-view technologies.

6.1 SYSTEM DESIGN:

Systems design is the process of defining the architecture, components, modules, interfaces, and data for a system to satisfy specified requirements. Systems design could be seen as the application of systems theory to product development. There is some overlap with the disciplines of systems analysis, systems architecture and systems engineering.

6.2 DATA FLOW DIAGRAM:

1. The DFD is also called as bubble chart. It is a simple graphical formalism that can be used to represent a system in terms of input data to the system, various processing carried out on this data, and the output data is generated by this system.

24

2. The data flow diagram (DFD) is one of the most important modeling tools. It is used to model the system components. These components are the system process, the data used by the process, an external entity that interacts with the system and the information flows in the system.

3. DFD shows how the information moves through the system and how it is modified by a series of transformations. It is a graphical technique that depicts information flow and the transformations that are applied as data moves from input to output.

4. DFD is also known as bubble chart. A DFD may be used to represent a system at any level of abstraction. DFD may be partitioned into levels that represent increasing information flow and functional detail.

6.2.1 REGISTRATION & LOGIN

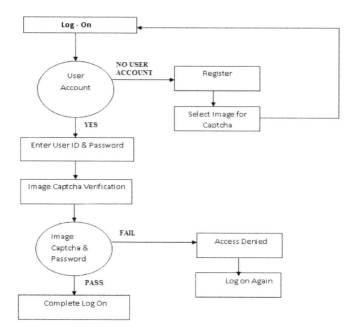

6.2.2 HOME PAGE

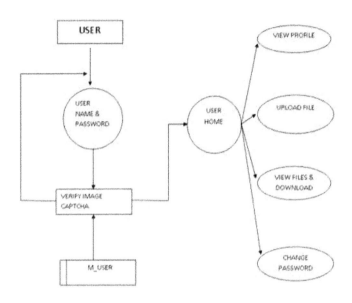

6.2.3 SETTING CAPTCHA TO UPLOAD FILES

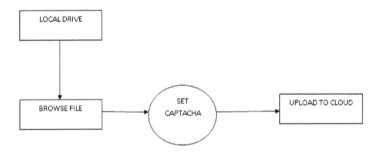

6.2.4 CAPTCHA VERIFICATION FOR DOWNLOADING FILES

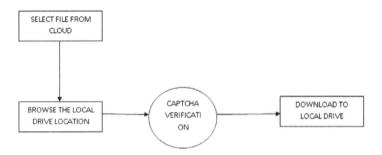

6.2.5 PROJECT SEQUENCE DIAGRAM

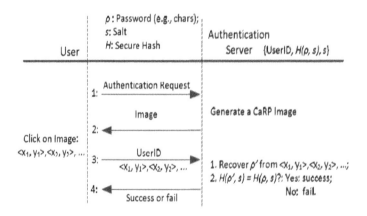

CaRP Authentication Flow Chart.

CHAPTER 7

MODULES DESCRIPTION

7.1 MODULES ELUCIDATION

The module elucidation provides a detailed preview of the system Captcha as a Graphical Password. It is provided with a user registration page where the user is allowed to register for the first time and he must be providing a click based password. So the users must be specifying with a Captcha password and also enters to the system. After registration the user can login and enter to the system which is been secured by a Graphical password. So the user wants to use a particular file then he should provide with an additional security called the Graphical password so that the system is more secure.

7.1.1 GRAPHICAL PASSWORD

In this module, Users are having authentication and security to access the detail which is presented in the Image system. Before accessing or searching the details user should have the account in that otherwise they should register first.

7.1.2 CAPTCHA IN AUTHENTICATION

It was introduced in to use both Captcha and password in a user authentication protocol, which we call Captcha-based Password Authentication (CbPA) protocol (Xiaoyuan Suo et al, 2005), to counter online dictionary attacks. The CbPA-protocol in requires solving a Captcha challenge after inputting a valid pair of user ID and password unless a valid browser cookie is received. For an invalid pair of user ID and password, the user has a certain probability to solve a Captcha challenge before being denied access.

7.1.3 THWART GUESSING ATTACKS

In a guessing attack, a password guess tested in an unsuccessful trial is determined wrong and excluded from subsequent trials. The number of undetermined password guesses decreases with more trials, leading to a better chance of finding the password. To counter guessing attacks, traditional approaches in designing graphical passwords aim at increasing the effective password space to make passwords harder to guess and thus require more trials. No matter how secure a graphical password

28

scheme is, the password can always be found by a brute force attack. In this paper, we distinguish two types of guessing.

Attacks: Automatic guessing attacks apply an automatic trial and error process but S can be manually constructed whereas human guessing attacks apply a manual trial and error process.

7.1.4 SECURITY OF UNDERLYING CAPTCHA

Computational intractability in recognizing objects in CaRP images is fundamental to CaRP. Existing analyses on Captcha security were mostly case by case or used an approximate process. No theoretic security model has been established yet. Object segmentation is considered as a computationally expensive, combinatorial-hard problem, which modern text Captcha schemes rely on.

CHAPTER 8

PERFORMANCE ANALYSIS

The comparison of different schemes are been presented in table 1 and 2 the * cell is been tested in real time environment and other cells are taken from previous researches. The WEKA Data Analysis Tool is used to derive the tables and graphs presented here. The usability features are been compared with various algorithms (Masrom. M et al, 2009) (Lashkari A.H et al, 2009) and for CaRP is studied and the results proves that our system is more efficient than other algorithms.

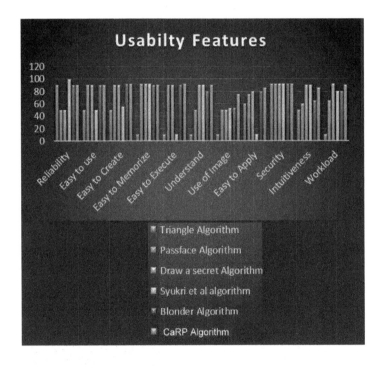

Figure 18. Representation of usability features with other algorithms

Attacks	Triangle Algorithm	Passface Algorithm	Draw a secret Algorithm	Syukri et al algorithm	Blonder Algorithm	CaRP*
Automatic Online Guessing Attacks	Yes	No	No	Yes	Yes	Yes
Human Guessing Attacks	No	No	No	Yes	No	Yes
Relay Attacks	Yes	No	No	No	Yes	Yes
Dictionary Attacks	Yes	Yes	Yes	Yes	Yes	Yes
Brute-force attack	Yes	Yes	No	Yes	Yes	Yes
Shoulder-Surfing Attacks	Yes	No	No	No	No	Yes

Table 1. Comparison of Attacks with other Algorithm

Usability features	Algorithms					
	Triangle Algorithm	Passface Algorithm	Draw a secret Algorithm	Syukri et al algorithm	Blonder Algorithm	CaRP*
Reliability	90	50	50	99	90	90
Easy to use	50	90	90	50	90	90
Easy to Create	50	90	90	55	92	92
Easy to Memorize	10	92	92	92	90	90
Easy to Execute	10	90	90	10	90	92
Easy to Understand	10	50	90	90	80	90
Use of Image	10	50	50	52	52	75
Easy to Apply	60	75	80	10	80	85
Security	92	92	92	92	92	92
Intuitiveness	50	60	90	90	65	85
Workload	10	65	92	80	80	90

Table 2. Comparison of Usability Features with other Algorithm

CHAPTER 9

CONCLUSION AND FUTURE ENHANCEMENTS

CaRP, has been proposed has a new security primitive relying on unsolved hard AI problems. CaRP is both a Captcha and a graphical password scheme. The notion of CaRP introduces a new family of graphical passwords, which adopts a new approach to counter online guessing attacks: a new CaRP image, which is also a Captcha challenge, is used for every login attempt to make trials of an online guessing attack computationally independent of each other (Zhu, B.B, et al, 2014). A password of CaRP can be found only probabilistically by automatic online guessing attacks including brute-force attacks, a desired security property that other graphical password schemes lack. Hotspots in CaRP images can no longer be exploited to mount automatic online guessing attacks, an inherent vulnerability in many graphical password systems. CaRP forces adversaries to resort to significantly less efficient and much more costly human-based attacks. In addition to offering protection from online guessing attacks, CaRP is also resistant to Captcha relay attacks, and, if combined with dual-view technologies, shoulder-surfing attacks. CaRP can also help reduce spam emails sent from a Web email service.

Our future work is to eradicate the shoulder surfing problems in the graphical passwords. When the graphical passwords are exposed several times in front of other persons it may lead to shoulder surfing problem i.e. the hacker may trace the password when we click the password in front of them for several times. So we aim to extend the CaRP by using different set images to confuse the hacker and thus improve the efficiency of the system.

REFERENCES

(R. Biddle et al, 2012)

R. Biddle, S. Chiasson, and P. C. van Oorschot, "Graphical passwords: Learning from the first twelve years," *ACM Comput. Surveys*, vol. 44, no. 4, 2012.

(Jermyn A. Mayer et al, 1999)

Jermyn, A. Mayer, F. Monrose, M. Reiter, and A. Rubin, "The design and analysis of graphical passwords," in *Proc. 8th USENIX Security Symp.*, 1999, pp. 1–15.

(H.Tao et al, 2008)

H. Tao and C. Adams, "Pass-Go: A proposal to improve the usability of graphical passwords," *Int. J. Netw. Security*, vol. 7, no. 2, pp. 273–292, 2008.

(S. Wiedenbeck et al, 2005)

S. Wiedenbeck, J. Waters, J. C. Birget, A. Brodskiy, and N. Memon, "PassPoints: Design and longitudinal evaluation of a graphical password system," *Int. J. HCI*, vol. 63, pp. 02–127, Jul. 2005.

(K.Golofit, 2007)

K. Golofit, "Click passwords under investigation," in *Proc. ESORICS*, 2007, pp. 343– 58.

(A. E. Dirik et al, 2007)

A. E. Dirik, N. Memon, and J.-C. Birget, "Modeling user choice in the passpoints graphical password scheme," in *Proc. Symp. Usable Privacy Security*, 2007, pp. 20–28.

(P. C. van Oorschot et al, 2008)

P. C. van Oorschot and J. Thorpe, "On predictive models and userdrawn graphical passwords," ACM Trans. Inf. Syst. Security, vol. 10, no. 4, pp. 1–33, 2008.

(J. Thorpe et al, 2007)

J. Thorpe and P. C. van Oorschot, "Human-seeded attacks and exploiting hot spots in graphical passwords," in Proc. USENIX Security, 2007, pp. 103–118.

(P. C. van Oorschot et al, 2010)

P. C. van Oorschot, A. Salehi-Abari, and J. Thorpe, "Purely automated attacks on passpoints-style graphical passwords," IEEE Trans. Inf. Forensics Security, vol. 5, no. 3, pp. 393–405, Sep. 2010.

(P. C. van Oorschot et al, 2011)

P. C. van Oorschot and J. Thorpe, "Exploiting predictability in clickbased graphical passwords," J. Comput. Security, vol. 19, no. 4, pp. 669–702, 2011.

(B. Pinkas et al, 2002)

B. Pinkas and T. Sander, "Securing passwords against dictionary attacks," in Proc. ACM CCS, 2002, pp. 161–170.

(P. C. van Oorschot et al, 2006)

P. C. van Oorschot and S. Stubblebine, "On countering online dictionary attacks with login histories and humans-in-the-loop," ACM Trans. Inf. Syst. Security, vol. 9, no. 3, pp. 235–258, 2006.

(M. Alsaleh et al, 2012)

M. Alsaleh, M. Mannan, and P. C. van Oorschot, "Revisiting defenses against large-scale online password guessing attacks," IEEE Trans. Dependable Secure Comput., vol. 9, no. 1, pp. 128–141, Jan./Feb. 2012.

(L. von Ahn et al, 2003)

L. von Ahn, M. Blum, N. J. Hopper, and J. Langford, "CAPTCHA: Using hard AI problems for security," in Proc. Eurocrypt, 2003, pp. 294–311.

(S. Chiasson et al, 2007)

S. Chiasson, P. C. van Oorschot, and R. Biddle, "Graphical password authentication using cued click points," in Proc. ESORICS, 2007, pp. 359–374.

(S. Chiasson et al, 2008)

S. Chiasson, A. Forget, R. Biddle, and P. C. van Oorschot, "Influencing users towards better passwords: Persuasive cued click-points," in Proc. Brit. HCI Group Annu. Conf. People Computer Culture, Creativity, Interaction, vol. 1. 2008, pp. 121–130.

(Masrom. M et al, 2009)

Masrom M., Towhidi F., Lashkari A.H. (2009) Pure and cued recall-based graphical user authentication, Application of Information and Communication Technologies (AICT).

(Lashkari A.H et al, 2009)

Lashkari A.H. and Farmand S. (2009) A survey on usability and security features in graphical user authentication algorithms International Journal of Computer Science and Network Security (IJCSNS), VOL.9 No.9, Singapore.

(Ahn,L. von et al, 2003)

Ahn, L. von, Blum, M., Hopper, N. J., & Langford, J., (2003), "CAPTCHA: Using hard AI problems for security", Proceedings of Eurocrypt 2003.

(Mukta Rao et al, 2012)

Mukta Rao and Nipur Singh "Random Handwritten CAPTCHA: Web Security with a Difference" I.J. Information Technology and Computer Science, 2012, 9, 53-58 Published Online August 2012 in MECS (http://www.mecs-press.org/) DOI: 10.5815/ijitcs.2012.09.07.

(Xiao Ling-Zi et al, 2012)

Xiao Ling-Zi and Zhang Yi-Chun "A Case Study of Text-Based CAPTCHA Attacks" cyber-Enabled Distributed Computing and Knowledge Discovery (CyberC), 2012 International Conference 10.1109/CyberC.2012.28.

(Xiaoyuan Suo et al, 2005)

Xiaoyuan Suo, Ying Zhu, Owen, G.S, "Graphical passwords: a survey" Computer Security Applications Conference, 21st Annual 5-9 Dec. 2005, 1063-9527, IEEE, Computer Security Application.

(Zhu, B.B et al, 2014)

Zhu, B.B, Yan, Guanbo Bao and Maowei Yang "Captcha as Graphical Passwords - A New Security Primitive Based on Hard AI Problems", IEEE Transactions on Information Forensics and Security, March 2014, pp: 891-904. DOI: 10.1109/TIFS.2014.2312547.

SCREEN SHOTS

HOME SCREEN:

REGISTRATION:

CLICK BASED IMAGE CAPTCHA:

REGISTRATION COMPLETED:

LOGIN:

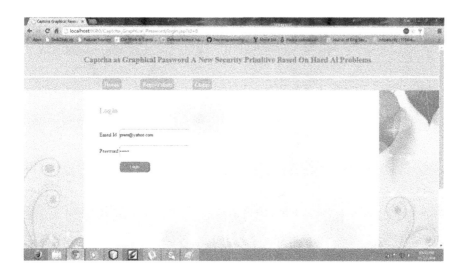

CAPTCHA FOR AUTHENTICATION:

INVALID CAPTCHA:

FILES UPLOADING:

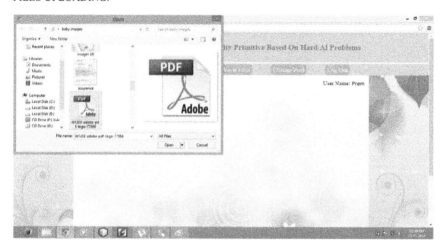

SETTING GRAPHICAL PASSWORD:

SUCCESSFULLY UPLOADED:

UPLOADED DOCUMENTS:

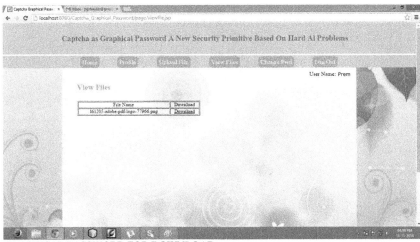

GRAPHICAL PASSWORD FOR DOWNLOAD:

DOWNLOAD SUCCESS:

APPENDIX – I
SOURCE CODE

```
<%@page import="java.sql.*" %>
<%@page import="c_grp.services.ServiceLocator"%>
<%@page import="java.sql.DriverManager"%>
<%@page import="java.sql.Statement"%>
<%@page contentType="text/html" pageEncoding="UTF-8"%>
```

HOMEPAGE CODE:

```
<!DOCTYPE html>
<!--
To change this license header, choose License Headers in Project Properties.
To change this template file, choose Tools | Templates
and open the template in the editor.
-->
<html>
  <head>
    <title>Captcha Graphical Password</title>
    <meta charset="UTF-8">
    <meta name="viewport" content="width=device-width">
    <link type="text/css" rel="stylesheet" href="css/style.css"/>
  </head>
  <body>
    <div class="header">
      <div class="title"><h2>Captcha as Graphical Password A New Security Primitive Based On Hard Al Problems</h2></div>
    </div>
    <div class="header1"></div>
    <div class="menu">
      <div class="title">
        <ul >
```

44

```html
        <li><a href="index.html">Home</a></li>
        <li><a href="register.jsp">Registration </a></li>
        <li><a href="loginhome.jsp">Login</a></li>
      </ul>
    </div>
  </div>
  <div class="wrapper">
    <img src="images/images.jpg" width="960px" height="550px"/>
  </div>
</body>
</html>
```

LOGIN CODE:

```html
<!DOCTYPE html>
<!--
To change this license header, choose License Headers in Project Properties.
To change this template file, choose Tools | Templates
and open the template in the editor.
-->
<html>
  <head>
    <title>Captcha Graphical Password</title>
    <meta charset="UTF-8">
    <meta name="viewport" content="width=device-width">
    <link type="text/css" rel="stylesheet" href="css/style.css"/>
  </head>
  <body>

    <%
      String id=request.getParameter("id");

    %>
```

45

```html
<div class="header">
    <div class="title"><h2>Captcha as Graphical Password A New Security Primitive Based On
Hard Al Problems</h2></div>
    </div>
<div class="header1"></div>
<div class="menu">
    <div class="title">
      <ul >
        <li class="active"><a href="index.html">Home</a></li>
        <li><a href="index.html">Registration </a></li>
        <li><a href="index.html">Login</a></li>
      </ul>
    </div>
</div>
<div class="wrap">
    <h3>Login </h3>
    <form action="<%=request.getContextPath()%>/login_process.jsp" method="post"
class="register">

    <table >
      <tr>
        <td><input type="hidden" name="id" value="<%=id%>"/></td>
      </tr>
      <tr>

        <td>Email Id</td>
        <td><input type="text" name="email" placeholder="Email Id" required="required"/></td>
      </tr>
      <tr>
        <td>Password</td>
```

```
        <td><input type="password" name="pwd" placeholder="Password"
required="required"/></td>
        </tr>

        <div class="submit">
          <tr>
            <td></td>
            <td><input type="submit" value="Login" style=" width: 100px; background-color:
#339900; color: #fff;"/>
            </tr>
          </div>


      </table>
      </form>
    </div>
  </body>
</html>
```

CAPTCHA PROCESS:

```
<%@page import="java.util.ArrayList"%>
<%@page import="java.util.Collections"%>
<!DOCTYPE html>
<!--
To change this license header, choose License Headers in Project Properties.
To change this template file, choose Tools | Templates
and open the template in the editor.
-->
<html>
  <head>
    <title>Captcha Graphical Password</title>
    <meta charset="UTF-8">
```

```html
<meta name="viewport" content="width=device-width">
<link type="text/css" rel="stylesheet" href="css/style.css"/>
</head>
<body>

<div class="header">
    <div class="title"><h2>Captcha as Graphical Password A New Security Primitive Based On
Hard Al Problems</h2></div>
    </div>
<div class="header1"></div>
<div class="menu">
  <div class="title">
    <ul >
      <li class="active"><a href="index.html">Home</a></li>
      <li><a href="index.html">Registration </a></li>
      <li><a href="index.html">Login</a></li>
    </ul>
  </div>
</div>
<div class="wrap">
  <%

    String name=request.getParameter("name");
    HttpSession sesion = request.getSession();
    session.setAttribute("name",name);
    System.out.println("SessionName:"+name) ;
  %>
  <div class="clear"></div>
  <h4>Image CAPTCHA for Click</h4>

    <div class="captcha">
```

```
<ul>
    <li><a href="cap.jsp?cap=Bat"><img src="captcha/bat.jpg" width="75px;"
height="60px;" ></a></li>
    <li><a href="cap.jsp?cap=Cat3"><img src="captcha/cat_ccc.jpg" width="75px;"
height="60px;" ></a></li>
    <li><a href="cap.jsp?cap=Butterfly"><img src="captcha/butterfly.jpg"width="75px;"
height="60px;" ></a></li>
    <li><a href="cap.jsp?cap=Cat0"><img src="captcha/cat.jpg" width="75px;"
height="60px;" ></a></li>
    <li><a href="cap.jsp?cap=Chick"><img src="captcha/chick.jpg" width="75px;"
height="60px;" ></a></li>
    <li><a href="cap.jsp?cap=cow"><img src="captcha/cow.jpg"width="75px;"
height="60px;" ></a></li>
    <li><a href="cap.jsp?cap=Deer"><img src="captcha/deer.jpg"width="75px;"
height="60px;" ></a></li>
    <li><a href="cap.jsp?cap=Duck"><img src="captcha/duck.jpg"width="75px;"
height="60px;" ></a></li>
    <li><a href="cap.jsp?cap=Deer2"><img src="captcha/deer_dd.jpg"width="75px;"
height="60px;" ></a></li>
    <li><a href="cap.jsp?cap=Horse6"><img src="captcha/horse_hhhhh.jpg"width="75px;"
height="60px;" ></a></li>
    <li><a href="cap.jsp?cap=Dog2"><img src="captcha/dog.jpg"width="75px;"
height="60px;" a></li>
    <li><a href="cap.jsp?cap=Lion1"><img src="captcha/lion_l.jpg"width="75px;"
height="60px;" ></a></li>
    <li><a href="cap.jsp?cap=Cat"><img src="captcha/cat_c.jpg"width="75px;"
height="60px;" ></a></li>
    <li><a href="cap.jsp?cap=Horse0"><img src="captcha/horse.jpg"width="75px;"
height="60px;" ></a></li>
```

```html
<li><a href="cap.jsp?cap=Dog4"><img src="captcha/dog_ddd.jpg"width="75px;" height="60px;" ></a></li>
<li><a href="cap.jsp?cap=Duck1"><img src="captcha/duck_d.jpg"width="75px;" height="60px;" ></a></li>
<li><a href="cap.jsp?cap=Chicken"><img src="captcha/chicken.jpg"width="75px;" height="60px;" ></a></li>
<li><a href="cap.jsp?cap=Duck3"><img src="captcha/duck_dd.jpg"width="75px;" height="60px;" ></a></li>
<li><a href="cap.jsp?cap=Elephant"><img src="captcha/elephant.jpg"width="75px;" height="60px;" ></a></li>
<li><a href="cap.jsp?cap=Fish7"><img src="captcha/fish.jpg"width="75px;" height="60px;" ></a></li>
<li><a href="cap.jsp?cap=Rabbit3"><img src="captcha/rabbit_rr.jpg"width="75px;" height="60px;" ></a></li>
<li><a href="cap.jsp?cap=Tiger"><img src="captcha/tiger_t.jpg"width="75px;" height="60px;" ></a></li>
<li><a href="cap.jsp?cap=Dog6"><img
<li><a href="cap.jsp?cap=Fly"><img src="captcha/fly.jpg"width="75px;" height="60px;" ></a></li>
<li><a href="cap.jsp?cap=fox"><img src="captcha/fox.jpg"width="75px;" height="60px;" ></a></li>
<li><a href="cap.jsp?cap=frog"><img src="captcha/frog.jpg"width="75px;" height="60px;" ></a></li>
<li><a href="cap.jsp?cap=Horse2"><img src="captcha/horse_h.jpg"width="75px;" height="60px;" ></a></li>
<li><a href="cap.jsp?cap=Chicking1"><img src="captcha/chicking.jpg"width="75px;" height="60px;" ></a></li>
<li><a href="cap.jsp?cap=Horse"><img src="captcha/horse_hh.jpg"width="75px;" height="60px;" ></a></li>
<li><a href="cap.jsp?cap=Fish2"><img src="captcha/fish_f.jpg"width="75px;" height="60px;"></a></li>
```

```html
<li><a href="cap.jsp?cap=Horse5"><img src="captcha/horse_hhhh.jpg"width="75px;" height="60px;" ></a></li>
<li><a href="cap.jsp?cap=Lion"><img src="captcha/lion.jpg"width="75px;" height="60px;" ></a></li>

<li><a href="cap.jsp?cap=Lizard"><img src="captcha/lizard.jpg"width="75px;" height="60px;" ></a></li>
<li><a href="cap.jsp?cap=Monkey"><img src="captcha/monkey.jpg"width="75px;" height="60px;" ></a></li>
<li><a href="cap.jsp?cap=Mouse"><img src="captcha/mouse.jpg"width="75px;" height="60px;" ></a></li>
<li><a href="cap.jsp?cap=Owl"><img src="captcha/owl.jpg"width="75px;" height="60px;" ></a></li>
<li><a href="cap.jsp?cap=Pandabeer"><img src="captcha/pandabeer.jpg"width="75px;" height="60px;" ></a></li>
<li><a href="cap.jsp?cap=Rabbit"><img src="captcha/rabbit_r.jpg"width="75px;" height="60px;" ></a></li>
<li><a href="cap.jsp?cap=Fish3"><img src="captcha/fish_ff.jpg"width="75px;" height="60px;" ></a></li>
<li><a href="cap.jsp?cap=Rabbit4"><img src="captcha/rabbit_rrr.jpg"width="75px;" height="60px;" ></a></li>
<li><a href="cap.jsp?cap=Dog"><img src="captcha/dog_dd.jpg"width="75px;" height="60px;" ></a></li>
<li><a href="cap.jsp?cap=Snail"><img src="captcha/snail.jpg"width="75px;" height="60px;" ></a></li>
<li><a href="cap.jsp?cap=squirrel1"><img src="captcha/squirrel.jpg"width="75px;" height="60px;"></a></li>
<li><a href="cap.jsp?cap=Dog5"><img src="captcha/dog_dddd.jpg"width="75px;" height="60px;" ></a></li>
<li><a href="cap.jsp?cap=Cat5"><img src="captcha/cat_cccc.jpg"width="75px;" height="60px;" ></a></li>
```

```html
            <li><a href="cap.jsp?cap=Squirrel"><img src="captcha/squirrel_s.jpg"width="75px;"
height="60px;" ></a></li>
                <li><a href="cap.jsp?cap=Tiger"><img src="captcha/tiger.jpg"width="75px;"
height="60px;" ></a></li>
                <li><a href="cap.jsp?cap=Deer1"><img src="captcha/deer_d.jpg"width="75px;"
height="60px;" ></a></li>
                <li><a href="cap.jsp?cap=Tiger2"><img src="captcha/tiger_tt.jpg"width="75px;"
height="60px;" ></a></li>
                <li><a href="cap.jsp?cap=Tortoise"><img src="captcha/tortoise.jpg"width="75px;"
height="60px;" ></a></li>
                <li><a href="cap.jsp?cap=Dog1"><img src="captcha/dog_d.jpg"width="75px;"
height="60px;" ></a></li>

    </ul>
        </div>
        </div>
        </body>
    </html>
```

APPENDIX- II

LIST OF PUBLICATIONS

1. V.Premanand[1], A.Meiappane[2] and V.Arulalan[3] Article: Survey on Captcha and its Techniques for BOT Protection. International Journal of Computer Applications 109(5):1-4, January 2015.